Delicious breakfasts

Delicious
breakfasts

Love Food is an imprint of Parragon Books Ltd

Parragon
Queen Street House
4 Queen Street
Bath BA1 1HE

Copyright © Parragon Books Ltd 2006

All rights reserved. No part of this publication may be reproduced, stored
in a retrieval system or transmitted, in any form or by any means, electronic,
mechanical, photocopying, recording or otherwise, without the prior permission
of the copyright holder.

Cover and internal design by Mark Cavanagh
Introduction by Bridget Jones
Photography by Don Last
Additional photography by Gunter Beer
Home Economist Christine Last

ISBN 978-1-4054-9640-7
Printed in China

Notes for reader
• This book uses metric and imperial measurements. Follow the same units of
measurements throughout; do not mix imperial and metric.
• All spoon measurements are level: teaspoons are assumed to be 5 ml and
tablespoons are assumed to be 15 ml.
• Unless otherwise stated, milk is assumed to be low fat and eggs are medium. The
times given are an approximate guide only.
• Some recipes contain nuts. If you are allergic to nuts you should avoid using them
and any products containing nuts. Recipes using raw or very lightly cooked eggs
should be avoided by infants, the elderly, pregnant women, convalescents and anyone
suffering from illness.

Contents

Breakfasts

Early bird or night owl, no matter when you feel energetic, breakfast is important for vitality. It will awaken your mind, re-balance your body, and provide energy and rejuvenating nutrients to keep you ahead of the morning and on track all day.

By morning, the body has digested yesterday's meals. Many people feel grumpy and lacklustre because their blood glucose levels have fallen overnight. Food and liquid raise blood glucose and prevent dehydration. Get into the breakfast habit and zing into life – there are lots of options and no excuses for missing out!

Personal best every day
This is lifestyle eating and it has to be just right. Key features of the best everyday breakfasts are familiarity, personal favourites, and practicality – they have to be quick and easy. Single people, couples, busy parents, children and teenagers have different takes on breakfast – weekends may bring room to manoeuvre but Monday to Friday has to run like clockwork! Everyone has to be fed, watered, and on the way, some older children can help feed themselves, and some adolescents need to be persuaded to eat (they *so* need to eat breakfast).

Food to keep going
The ideal combination is some fast-acting source of energy for a wide-awake buzz (a large glass of juice is great) backed up by slow-release foods that will provide fuel until the next meal. Generally, morning food is designed to get you going with minimum effort and maximum return – cereals, toast and marmalade, fruit and yogurt.

Carbohydrates are important, especially the type that break down slowly, releasing energy over a few hours. Those are the complex carbohydrates – starches rather than sugars. The glycaemic index is a scale that rates

the speed with which carbohydrates are broken down and absorbed compared to glucose. It gives values of 0–100 known as GI values. The higher the value, the quicker the food is absorbed (glucose has a value of 100). Eating slow-release foods (low GI value) helps to avoid the hunger pangs and lack of energy.

High-fibre foods that are not highly processed (and not high sugar) provide energy for a few hours. Bran cereals and porridge oats are low GI and tortilla wraps, croissants and wholemeal bread are medium GI (stoneground wholemeal bread is low GI). Apples, pears, grapefruit, oranges, grapes, berries and bananas that are not too ripe are all low GI. Combining slow-release foods with others that provide instant energy slows down the energy rush. Fats and proteins slow down the process. Poached eggs, tomatoes and mushrooms with toast, followed by fruit, is a good mix. Homemade muesli is excellent – oats, grains, nuts, dried fruit, with milk, provide a great mix of nutrients, with 'good'

fat and protein from nuts, minerals and vitamins, especially if served with berries, apple or mango.

All days: all sorts

Breakfast is wonderfully versatile – savoury or sweet, delicate or substantial, food can be formal or on the move.

It's good to eat a variety of breakfasts – cereals some days; eggs on toast followed by fruit; yogurt with fruit, nuts and seeds; or toasted waffles with banana, nuts and yogurt. When time is tight, a smoothie can be whizzed and drunk in seconds (or prepared ahead).

Time to indulge

On birthday weekends, bank holidays, when friends stay, for an anniversary or Christmas...indulgent breakfasts are superlative! Scrambled eggs with smoked salmon, a classic cooked breakfast, or what about sweet treats, such as pancakes or warm croissants with home-made jam?

Rise & Shine

serves 2

3 large ripe sweetie
grapefruit or ugli fruit

150ml/5 fl oz sparkling water

1 tbsp runny honey (optional)

some slices of lime or peeled
kiwi fruit

2 tbsp yogurt

wake up sweetie

Halve the sweetie grapefruit and the ugli fruit and squeeze into
two glasses.

Add water and honey if liked.

Serve with a slice or two of lime or kiwi, floated on the surface
and topped with a spoonful of yogurt.

serves 2

250 ml/9 fl oz carrot juice

4 tomatoes, skinned,
deseeded and roughly
chopped

1 tbsp lemon juice

25 g/1 oz fresh parsley

1 tbsp grated fresh root
ginger

6 ice cubes

125 ml/4 fl oz water

chopped fresh parsley,
to garnish

carrot & ginger energizer

Put the carrot juice, tomatoes and lemon juice into a food processor and process gently until combined.

Add the parsley to the food processor along with the ginger and ice cubes. Process until well combined, then pour in the water and process until smooth.

Pour the mixture into glasses and garnish with chopped fresh parsley. Serve at once.

serves 2

250 ml/9 fl oz carrot juice

250 ml/9 fl oz tomato juice

2 large red peppers, deseeded
and roughly chopped

1 tbsp lemon juice

freshly ground black pepper

carrot & red pepper booster

Pour the carrot juice and tomato juice into a food processor and process gently until combined.

Add the red peppers and lemon juice. Season with plenty of freshly ground black pepper and process until smooth.

Pour the mixture into tall glasses, add straws and serve.

serves 2

2 large ripe Williams or
similar juicy pears

juice of 4 medium oranges

4 cubes crystallized ginger

pear, orange & ginger reviver

Peel and quarter the pears, removing the cores. Put into a food processor with the orange juice and the crystallized ginger and process until smooth.

Pour into glasses and serve.

serves 2

1 wedge of watermelon,
weighing about 350 g/12 oz

ice cubes

1–2 fresh mint sprigs,
to garnish

watermelon refresher

Cut the rind off the watermelon. Chop the watermelon into
chunks, discarding any seeds.

Put the watermelon chunks into a food processor and process
until smooth.

Place ice cubes in two glasses. Pour the watermelon mixture
over the ice and serve garnished with the mint.

serves 2–3

125 g/4^1/$_2$ oz whole blanched
almonds

600 ml/1 pint milk

2 ripe bananas, halved

1 tsp natural vanilla extract

ground cinnamon,
for sprinkling

almond & banana smoothie

Put the almonds into a food processor and process until very finely chopped.

Add the milk, bananas and vanilla extract and blend until smooth and creamy. Pour into glasses and sprinkle with cinnamon.

serves 1

1 banana, sliced

85 g/3 oz fresh strawberries, hulled

150 g/5^1/$_2$ oz natural yogurt

banana & strawberry smoothie

Put the banana, strawberries and yogurt into a food processor or blender and process for a few seconds until smooth.

Pour into a glass and serve immediately.

serves 1

25 g/1 oz blueberries

85 g/3 oz raspberries, thawed
if frozen

1 tsp clear honey

200 ml/7 fl oz live or
bio yogurt

about 1 heaped tbsp
crushed ice

1 tbsp sesame seeds

berry smoothie

Put the blueberries into a food processor or blender and process
for 1 minute.

Add the raspberries, honey and yogurt and process for a further
minute.

Add the ice and sesame seeds and process again for a further
minute.

Pour into a tall glass and serve immediately.

serves 2

250 ml/9 fl oz orange juice

125 ml/4 fl oz natural yogurt

2 eggs

2 bananas, sliced and frozen

slice of fresh banana,
to garnish

breakfast smoothie

Pour the orange juice and yogurt into a food processor and process gently until combined.

Add the eggs and frozen bananas and process until smooth.

Pour the mixture into glasses and garnish the rims with a slice of fresh banana.

serves 2

2 ripe bananas

200 ml/7 fl oz crème fraîche

125 ml/4 fl oz milk

2 tbsp clear honey, plus extra
for drizzling

1/2 tsp vanilla essence

banana breakfast shake

Put the bananas, crème fraîche, milk, honey and vanilla essence into a food processor and process until smooth.

Pour into glasses and serve at once, drizzled with a little more honey.

Healthy Start

serves 4

115 g/4 oz ready-to-eat dried peaches

85 g/3 oz ready-to-eat dried apricots

55 g/2 oz ready-to-eat dried pineapple chunks

55 g/2 oz ready-to-eat dried mango slices

225 ml/8 fl oz unsweetened clear apple juice

4 tbsp low-fat natural yogurt (optional)

exotic dried fruit compote

Put the dried fruit into a small saucepan with the apple juice. Bring slowly to the boil, then reduce the heat to low, cover and simmer for 10 minutes.

Spoon into serving dishes and top each serving with a tablespoon of yogurt, if desired. Serve immediately.

serves 4

1 pink grapefruit

1 yellow grapefruit

3 oranges

citrus zing

Using a sharp knife, carefully cut away all the peel and pith from the grapefruit and oranges.

Working over a bowl to catch the juice, carefully cut the grapefruit and orange segments between the membranes to obtain skinless segments of fruit. Discard any pips. Add the segments to the bowl and gently mix together.

Cover and refrigerate until required or divide between 4 serving dishes and serve immediately.

serves 2

1 small charentais,
cantaloupe or galia melon

2 kiwi fruit

melon & kiwi fruit bowl

Cut the melon into quarters and remove and discard the seeds. Remove the melon flesh from the skin with a sharp knife and cut into chunks, or if you have a melon baller, scoop out as much of the melon flesh as possible and place in a bowl.

Peel the kiwi fruit and cut the flesh into slices. Add to the melon and gently mix together. Cover and refrigerate until required or divide between 2 serving dishes and serve immediately.

serves 4

3 tbsp clear honey

100 g/3^{1}/$_{2}$ oz mixed
unsalted nuts

8 tbsp Greek yogurt

200 g/7 oz fresh blueberries

greek yogurt with honey, nuts & blueberries

Heat the honey in a small saucepan over a medium heat, add the nuts and stir until they are well coated. Remove from the heat and leave to cool slightly.

Divide the yogurt between 4 serving bowls, then spoon over the nut mixture and blueberries.

serves 2

100 g/3^1/$_2$ oz jumbo oats

200 ml/7 fl oz apple juice

1 red apple, cored

1 tbsp lemon juice

25 g/1 oz toasted hazelnuts, chopped

^{1}/$_2$ tsp ground cinnamon

100 ml/3^1/$_2$ fl oz natural bio yogurt

2 tbsp runny honey (optional)

70 g/2^1/$_2$ oz fresh bilberries or blueberries

bilberry bircher muesli

Put the oats and apple juice in a bowl, cover with clingfilm and leave to soak in the refrigerator for an hour. You can do this the night before.

Grate or chop the apple and mix with the lemon juice to prevent discoloration.

Add the apple, hazelnuts and cinnamon onto the oat mixture and mix well.

Spoon the mixture into serving bowls and top with the yogurt. Drizzle over the honey, if using. Spoon the bilberries over the muesli and serve.

serves 4

for the granola

10 g/¼ oz rolled oats

5 g/⅛ oz sesame seeds

pinch of ground ginger

5 g/⅛ oz sunflower seeds

2 tsp freshly squeezed
orange juice

1 tsp runny honey

for the fruit cocktail

300 g/10½ oz deseeded
watermelon, cut into chunks

100 g/3½ oz fresh orange
segments

6 tbsp freshly squeezed
orange juice

1 tsp finely grated orange
zest

1 tsp peeled and finely sliced
root ginger

1 tsp runny honey

½ tsp arrowroot, blended
with a little cold water

watermelon, orange & ginger cocktail with granola

Preheat the oven to 180°C/350°F/Gas Mark 4.

To make the granola, put all the dry ingredients into a bowl, then add the orange juice and honey and mix thoroughly. Spread out on a non-stick baking tray and bake for 7–8 minutes. Remove from the oven, break up into pieces, then return to the oven for a further 7–8 minutes. Remove from the oven and break up again. Leave to cool on the baking sheet. The mixture will become crunchy when cool.

To make the fruit cocktail, put the watermelon and orange segments into a bowl. Put the orange juice and zest, ginger and honey into a small saucepan over a medium heat and bring to the boil. Gradually stir in the arrowroot mixture and cook, stirring constantly, until thickened.

Pour the mixture over the fruit and leave to cool. Cover and chill in the fridge.

Spoon the fruit into glasses and sprinkle over the granola.

serves 4

12 large portobello mushrooms, wiped over and stems removed

2 tbsp sunflower oil, plus extra for oiling

1 fennel bulb, stalks removed, finely chopped

100 g/3½ oz sun-dried tomatoes, finely chopped

2 garlic cloves, crushed

125 g/4½ oz grated fontina cheese

50 g/1¾ oz freshly grated Parmesan cheese

3 tbsp chopped fresh basil

salt and pepper

1 tbsp olive oil

fresh Parmesan cheese shavings

1 tbsp chopped fresh parsley

stuffed portobello mushrooms with shaved parmesan

Preheat the oven to 180°C/350°F/Gas Mark 4. Lightly oil a large ovenproof dish. Place 8 of the mushrooms, cup-side up, in the dish and chop the remaining 4 mushrooms finely.

Heat the sunflower oil in a non-stick frying pan, add the chopped mushrooms, fennel, sun-dried tomatoes and garlic and cook over a low heat until the vegetables are soft but not browned. Remove from the heat and leave to cool.

When cool, add the grated cheeses, basil and salt and pepper to taste. Mix well. Brush the mushrooms lightly with the olive oil and fill each cavity with a spoonful of the vegetable filling. Bake for 20–25 minutes, or until the mushrooms are tender and the filling is heated through.

Top with Parmesan shavings and parsley and serve immediately, allowing 2 mushrooms for each person.

serves 4

300 g/10¹/2 oz asparagus, trimmed

1 tbsp white wine vinegar

4 large eggs

85 g/3 oz Parmesan cheese

pepper

asparagus with poached eggs & parmesan

Bring 2 saucepans of water to the boil. Add the asparagus to one saucepan, return to a simmer and cook for 5 minutes, or until just tender.

Meanwhile, to poach the eggs, reduce the heat of the second saucepan to a simmer and add the vinegar. When the water is barely simmering, carefully break the eggs into the saucepan. Poach the eggs for 3 minutes, or until the whites are just set but the yolks are still soft.

Drain the asparagus and divide between 4 warmed plates. Top each plate of asparagus with an egg and shave over the cheese. Season to taste with pepper and serve immediately.

serves 4

225 g/8 oz broccoli

1 tbsp white wine vinegar

4 eggs

225 g/8 oz smoked salmon

for the dressing

150 ml/5 fl oz 8% fat fromage frais

1–1¹/₂ tsp Dijon mustard

2 tsp snipped fresh chives

wholemeal or Granary bread, to serve

smoked salmon with broccoli & poached eggs

Divide the broccoli into spears then cook in boiling water for 5–6 minutes, or until tender. Drain and keep warm while you poach the eggs.

To poach the eggs, fill a saucepan three-quarters full with water and bring to a boil over low heat. Reduce the heat to a simmer and add the vinegar. When the water is barely simmering, carefully break the eggs into the saucepan. Poach the eggs for 3 minutes, or until the whites are just set but the yolks are still soft.

Meanwhile, divide the smoked salmon between four individual plates. Stir all the dressing ingredients together in a mixing jug until blended.

Place the broccoli spears on the plates, top each serving with a poached egg, spoon over a little dressing and serve with wholemeal or Granary bread.

serves 4

1 tbsp olive oil

3 shallots, finely chopped

500 g/1 lb 2 oz baby spinach
leaves

4 tbsp single cream

freshly grated nutmeg

pepper

4 large eggs

4 tbsp Parmesan cheese,
finely grated

baked eggs with spinach

Preheat the oven to 200°C/400°F/Gas Mark 6. Heat the oil in a frying pan over a medium heat, add the shallots and cook, stirring frequently, for 4–5 minutes, or until soft. Add the spinach, cover and cook for 2–3 minutes, or until the spinach has wilted. Remove the lid and cook until all the liquid has evaporated.

Add the cream to the spinach and season to taste with nutmeg and pepper. Spread the spinach mixture over the base of 4 shallow gratin dishes and make a well in the mixture with the back of a spoon.

Crack an egg into each well and scatter over the cheese. Bake in the preheated oven for 10–12 minutes, or until the eggs are set. Serve at once.

The
Big Breakfast

serves 4

1 tbsp white wine vinegar

4 eggs

4 English muffins

4 slices good-quality ham

for the quick hollandaise
sauce

3 egg yolks

200 g/7 oz butter

1 tbsp lemon juice

pepper

eggs benedict with quick hollandaise sauce

To poach the eggs, fill a pan three-quarters full with water and bring to a boil over low heat. Reduce the heat to a simmer and add the vinegar. When the water is barely simmering, carefully break the eggs into the pan. Poach the eggs for 3 minutes, or until the whites are just set but the yolks are still soft.

Meanwhile, to make the hollandaise sauce, place the egg yolks in a blender or food processor. Melt the butter in a small saucepan until bubbling. With the motor running, gradually add the hot butter to the blender in a steady stream until the sauce is thick and creamy. Add the lemon juice, and a little warm water if the sauce is too thick, then season to taste with pepper. Remove from the blender or food processor and keep warm.

Split the muffins and toast them on both sides. To serve, top each muffin with a slice of ham, a poached egg and a generous spoonful of hollandaise sauce.

serves 2

300 g/10½ oz button mushrooms

15 g/½ oz butter

1 tbsp vegetable oil

salt and pepper

1 small red chilli, deseeded and finely chopped

1 tbsp soured cream

2 tbsp chopped fresh parsley

1 tbsp chopped fresh rosemary

slices of ciabatta bread, toasted

extra-virgin olive oil

handful of rocket leaves

mushrooms with rosemary, chilli, soured cream & rocket

Wipe the mushrooms with a damp cloth and slice thinly.

Heat the butter and vegetable oil in a wide sauté pan and add the mushrooms, stirring until well coated. Season lightly with salt and pepper and add the chopped chilli. Cover and cook for 1–2 minutes, or until the mushrooms have softened, then stir in the soured cream. Sprinkle over the chopped parsley and rosemary.

Serve with slices of toasted ciabatta, drizzled lightly with olive oil, topped with a few rocket leaves.

serves 2

4 eggs

100 ml/3½ fl oz single cream

salt and pepper

2 tbsp snipped fresh chives,
plus 4 whole fresh chives
to garnish

25 g/1 oz butter

4 slices brioche loaf,
lightly toasted

chive scrambled eggs with brioche

Break the eggs into a medium bowl and whisk gently with the cream. Season to taste with salt and pepper and add the snipped chives.

Melt the butter in a non stick pan over medium heat, pour in the egg mixture, and cook, stirring gently with a wooden spoon, for 5–6 minutes, or until lightly set.

Place the toasted brioche slices in the centre of 2 plates and spoon over the scrambled eggs. Serve immediately, garnished with fresh chives.

makes 6 soufflés

55 g/2 oz butter, plus extra,
melted, for greasing

40 g/1½ oz plain flour

150 ml/5 fl oz milk

250 g/9 oz ricotta cheese

4 egg yolks

2 tbsp finely chopped
fresh parsley

2 tbsp finely chopped
fresh thyme

1 tbsp finely chopped
fresh rosemary

salt and pepper

6 egg whites

200 ml/7 fl oz single cream

6 tbsp grated Parmesan
cheese

sautéed button mushrooms,
to serve

cheese & herb soufflés with sautéed mushrooms

Preheat the oven to 180°C/350°F/Gas Mark 4. Brush six 9-cm/ 3½-inch soufflé dishes well with melted butter and set aside. Melt the butter in a medium saucepan, add the flour and cook for 30 seconds, stirring constantly. Whisk in the milk and continue whisking over a low heat until the mixture thickens. Cook for a further 30 seconds. Remove from the heat and beat in the ricotta. Add the egg yolks and herbs and season well with salt and pepper.

Beat the egg whites in a clean bowl until they form stiff peaks then gently fold them through the ricotta mixture. Spoon into the prepared dishes, filling them just to the top. Place in a baking dish and pour in enough boiling water to come halfway up the sides of the dishes. Bake for 15–20 minutes, or until the soufflés are well risen and browned. Remove from the oven, leave to cool for 10 minutes, then gently ease out of their moulds. Place in a lightly greased ovenproof dish and cover with clingfilm.

Increase the oven temperature to 200°C/400°F/Gas Mark 6. Remove the clingfilm and pour the cream evenly over the soufflés, sprinkle with Parmesan and return to the oven for a further 15 minutes. Serve immediately with sautéed mushrooms.

serves 4

8 eggs

90 ml/3 fl oz single cream

2 tbsp chopped fresh dill, plus extra

salt and pepper

100 g/3½ oz smoked salmon, cut into small pieces

25 g/1 oz butter

slices rustic bread, toasted

sprig of dill, to garnish

scrambled eggs with smoked salmon

Break the eggs into a large bowl and whisk together with the cream and dill. Season to taste with salt and pepper. Add the smoked salmon and mix to combine.

Melt the butter in a large non-stick frying pan and pour in the egg and smoked salmon mixture. Using a wooden spatula, gently scrape the egg away from the sides of the pan as it begins to set and swirl the pan slightly to allow the uncooked egg to fill the surface.

When the eggs are almost cooked but still creamy, remove from the heat and spoon onto the prepared toast. Serve immediately, garnished with a sprig of dill.

makes 6 parcels

150 g/5¹/2 oz feta cheese, crumbled

250 g/9 oz ricotta cheese

150 g/5¹/2 oz smoked salmon, diced

2 tbsp chopped fresh dill

2 tbsp snipped fresh chives

salt and pepper

12 sheets filo pastry

100 g/3¹/2 oz butter, melted, plus extra for greasing

4 tbsp dried breadcrumbs

6 tsp fennel seeds

smoked salmon, feta & dill filo parcels

Preheat the oven to 180°C/350°F/Gas Mark 4. Lightly grease a baking tray. In a large bowl, combine the feta, ricotta, smoked salmon, dill and chives. Season to taste with pepper.

Lay out a sheet of pastry on your work surface and brush well with melted butter. Sprinkle over 2 teaspoons of the breadcrumbs and cover with a second sheet of pastry. Brush with butter and spread a large tablespoon of the salmon mixture on one end of the pastry. Roll the pastry up, folding in the sides, to enclose the salmon completely and create a neat parcel. Place on the prepared baking tray, brush the top of the parcel with butter and sprinkle over 1 teaspoon of the fennel seeds. Repeat with the remaining ingredients to make 6 parcels.

Bake the parcels for 25–30 minutes, or until the pastry is golden brown. Serve the parcels warm.

serves 2–4

115 g/4 oz cooked peeled prawns, thawed if frozen

4 spring onions, chopped

55 g/2 oz courgette, grated

4 eggs, separated

few dashes of Tabasco sauce, to taste

3 tbsp milk

salt and pepper

1 tbsp sunflower or olive oil

25 g/1 oz mature Cheddar cheese, grated

fluffy prawn omelette

Pat the prawns dry with kitchen paper, then mix with the spring onions and courgette in a bowl and reserve.

Using a fork, beat the egg yolks with the Tabasco, milk and salt and pepper to taste in a separate bowl.

Using an electric mixer or hand whisk, whisk the egg whites in a clean bowl until stiff peaks form. Gently stir the egg yolk mixture into the egg whites, taking care not to over-mix.

Heat the oil in a large, non-stick frying pan and when hot pour in the egg mixture. Cook over a low heat for 4–6 minutes, or until lightly set. Meanwhile, preheat the grill.

Spoon the prawn mixture on top of the eggs and sprinkle with the cheese. Cook under the preheated grill for 2–3 minutes, or until set and the top is golden brown. Cut into wedges and serve immediately.

makes 12 pastries

butter, for greasing

500 g/1 lb 2 oz prepared shortcrust pastry

plain flour, for rolling

2 tbsp wholegrain mustard

12 streaky bacon rashers, diced, cooked and drained well

12 small eggs

pepper

125 g/4$^{1}/_{2}$ oz grated Cheddar cheese

2 tbsp chopped fresh parsley

mini bacon & egg pastries with cheddar

Preheat the oven to 180°C/350°F/Gas Mark 4. Lightly grease a deep 12-cup muffin tin.

Roll the pastry out to a 5-mm/¼-inch thickness on a lightly floured work surface and cut out 12 circles approximately 13 cm/ 5 inches in diameter. Use to line the cups of the muffin tin, gently pleating the sides of the dough as you ease it into the moulds. Place ½ teaspoon of the mustard into the base of each pastry case and top with a little of the bacon.

Break an egg into a cup, spoon the yolk into the pastry case, then add enough of the white to fill the pastry case about two-thirds full. Do not overfill. Season to taste with pepper and sprinkle the grated cheese evenly over the tops of the pastries. Bake for 20–25 minutes, or until the egg is set and the cheese is golden brown.

Serve warm, sprinkled with chopped parsley.

serves 6

2 red peppers, halved and deseeded

2 small chorizo sausages, diced

1 tbsp olive oil

2 potatoes, peeled and diced

handful of fresh basil leaves, torn into pieces

6 large eggs, lightly beaten

6 tbsp grated Manchego cheese

salt and pepper

tortilla with roasted peppers & spicy chorizo

Preheat the oven to 200°C/400°F/Gas Mark 6. Place the red peppers on a lined baking tray and roast for 15 minutes, or until the skins are black. Remove from the oven and cover with a tea towel until cool. When cool, peel away the skins and dice the flesh.

Meanwhile, cook the diced chorizo in a 30-cm/12-inch non-stick frying pan until it is brown and the fat is rendered. Drain on kitchen paper. Wipe out the frying pan, then heat the oil and cook the diced potatoes for 5 minutes, or until soft and lightly browned. Return the chorizo to the pan with the potatoes and add the diced red peppers and torn basil leaves.

Mix the eggs and grated cheese together and season to taste with salt and pepper. Pour over the ingredients in the frying pan, using a wooden spoon to distribute the ingredients evenly. Leave to cook for a few minutes over a low heat until the egg has begun to set. To finish the tortilla, place the pan under a hot preheated grill to brown lightly.

Slide onto a serving plate and cut into wedges to serve.

serves 4

8 lean back bacon rashers

2 beef or 4 medium
tomatoes, halved

4 eggs

3 tbsp milk

salt and pepper

1 tbsp snipped fresh chives

1 tbsp unsalted butter

bacon & tomato scramble

Preheat the grill to high and cover the grill rack with foil.
Arrange the bacon on the foil and cook under the preheated grill
for 3–4 minutes on each side, or until crisp. About 3 minutes
before the end of cooking time, add the tomatoes, cut-side up,
and cook for the remainder of the cooking time.

Meanwhile, beat the eggs, milk and salt and pepper to taste in a
medium-size bowl, then stir in the chives.

Melt the butter in a non-stick saucepan over a medium heat,
pour in the egg mixture and cook, stirring gently with a wooden
spoon, for 5–6 minutes, or until lightly set.

Arrange the egg scramble with the cooked bacon and tomatoes
on warmed serving plates and serve immediately.

Sweet Treats

makes 12 waffles
to serve 4–6

175 g/6 oz plain flour

2 tsp baking powder

1/2 tsp salt

2 tsp caster sugar

2 eggs, separated

250 ml/9 fl oz milk

85 g/3 oz butter, melted

100 g/3 1/2 oz butter,
cut into pieces

3 tbsp golden syrup

3 large ripe bananas, peeled
and thickly sliced

waffles with caramelized bananas

Mix the flour, baking powder, salt and sugar together in a bowl. Whisk the egg yolks, milk and melted butter together with a fork, then stir this mixture into the dry ingredients to make a smooth batter.

Using an electric mixer or hand whisk, whisk the egg whites in a clean bowl until stiff peaks form. Fold into the batter mixture. Spoon 2 large tablespoons of the batter into a preheated waffle maker and cook according to the manufacturer's instructions.

To make the caramelized bananas, melt the butter with the golden syrup in a saucepan over a low heat and stir until combined. Leave to simmer for a few minutes until the caramel thickens and darkens slightly. Add the bananas and mix gently to coat. Pour over the warm waffles and serve immediately.

*makes 18 pancakes
to serve 4–6*

200 g/7 oz self-raising flour

100 g/3½ oz caster sugar

1 tsp ground cinnamon

1 egg

200 ml/7 fl oz milk

2 apples, peeled and grated

1 tsp butter

for the maple strup

85 g/3 oz butter, softened

3 tbsp maple syrup

apple pancakes with maple syrup butter

Mix the flour, sugar and cinnamon together in a bowl and make a well in the centre. Beat the egg and the milk together and pour into the well. Using a wooden spoon, gently incorporate the dry ingredients into the liquid until well combined, then stir in the grated apple.

Melt 1 tsp butter in a large non-stick frying pan over a low heat until melted and bubbling. Add tablespoons of the pancake mixture to form 9-cm/3½-inch circles. Cook each pancake for about 1 minute, until it starts to bubble lightly on the top and looks set, then flip it over and cook the other side for 30 seconds, or until cooked through. The pancakes should be golden brown; if not, increase the heat a little. Remove from the pan and keep warm. Repeat the process until all of the pancake batter has been uscd up (it is not necessary to add extra butter).

To make the maple syrup butter, melt the remaining butter with the maple syrup in a saucepan over a low heat and stir until combined. To serve, place the pancakes on serving dishes and spoon over the flavoured butter. Serve warm.

makes 10–12

140 g/5 oz plain flour

2 tbsp caster sugar

2 tsp baking powder

$^1/_2$ tsp salt

225 ml/8 fl oz buttermilk

3 tbsp butter, melted

1 large egg

140 g/5 oz fresh blueberries,
plus extra to garnish

sunflower or corn oil,
for oiling

butter

warm maple syrup

blueberry pancakes

Preheat the oven to 140°C/275°F/Gas Mark 1. Sieve the flour, sugar, baking powder and salt together into a large bowl and make a well in the centre.

Beat the buttermilk, butter and egg together in a separate small bowl, then pour the mixture into the well in the dry ingredients. Beat the dry ingredients into the liquid, gradually drawing them in from the side, until a smooth batter is formed. Gently stir in the blueberries.

Heat a large frying pan over a medium-high heat until a splash of water dances on the surface. Using a pastry brush or crumpled piece of kitchen paper, oil the base of the frying pan.

Drop about 4 tablespoons of batter separately into the frying pan and spread each out into a 10-cm/4-inch round. Continue adding as many pancakes as will fit in your frying pan. Cook until small bubbles appear on the surface, then flip over with a spatula or palette knife and cook the pancakes on the other side for a further 1–2 minutes until the bases are golden brown.

Transfer the pancakes to a warmed plate and keep warm in the preheated oven while you cook the remaining batter, lightly oiling the frying pan as before. Make a stack of the pancakes with baking paper in between each pancake.

Serve stacks of pancakes with a knob of butter on top, warm maple syrup for pouring and garnished with blueberries.

makes 8–10

115 g/4 oz plain flour

25 g/1 oz cocoa powder

pinch of salt

1 egg

25 g/1 oz caster sugar

350 ml/12 fl oz milk

50 g/1¾ oz butter

icing sugar, for dusting

ice cream or pouring cream, to serve

for the berry compote

150 g/5½ oz fresh blackberries

150 g/5½ oz fresh blueberries

225 g/8 oz fresh raspberries

55 g/2 oz caster sugar

juice of ½ lemon

½ tsp mixed spice (optional)

chocolate pancakes with berry compote

Preheat the oven to 140°C/275°F/Gas Mark 1. Sift the flour, cocoa powder and salt together into a large bowl and make a well in the centre.

Beat the egg, sugar and half the milk together in a separate bowl, then pour the mixture into the dry ingredients. Beat the dry ingredients into the liquid, gradually drawing them in from the side, until a smooth batter is formed. Gradually beat in the remaining milk. Pour the batter into a jug.

Heat an 18-cm/7-inch non-stick frying pan over a medium heat and add 1 teaspoon of the butter.

When the butter has melted, pour in enough batter just to cover the base, then swirl it round the pan while tilting it so that you have a thin, even layer. Cook for 30 seconds and then lift up the edge of the pancake to check if it is cooked. Loosen the pancake around the edge, then flip it over with a spatula or palette knife. Alternatively, toss the pancake by flipping the frying pan quickly with a flick of the wrist and catching it carefully. Cook on the other side until the base is golden brown.

Transfer the pancake to a warmed plate and keep warm in the preheated oven while you cook the remaining batter, adding the remaining butter to the frying pan as necessary. Make a stack of the pancakes with baking paper in between each pancake.

To make the compote, pick over the berries and put in a saucepan with the sugar, lemon juice and mixed spice, if using. Cook over a low heat until the sugar has dissolved and the berries are warmed through. Do not overcook.

Put a pancake on a warmed serving plate and spoon some of the compote onto the centre. Either roll or fold the pancake and dust with icing sugar. Repeat with the remaining pancakes. Serve with ice cream or pouring cream.

serves 4

4 eggs, plus 1 extra egg white

1/4 tsp ground cinnamon

1/4 tsp mixed spice

85 g/3 oz caster sugar

50 ml/2 fl oz freshly squeezed orange juice

300 g/10 1/2 oz mixed fresh seasonal berries, such as strawberries, raspberries and blueberries, picked over and hulled

4 slices thick white bread

1 tbsp butter, melted

fresh mint sprigs, to decorate

spiced french toast with seasonal berries

Preheat the oven to 220°C/425°F/Gas Mark 7. Put the eggs and egg white in a large, shallow bowl or dish and whisk together with a fork. Add the cinnamon and mixed spice and whisk until combined.

To prepare the berries, put the sugar and orange juice in a saucepan and bring to the boil over a low heat, stirring until the sugar has dissolved. Add the berries, remove from the heat and leave to cool for 10 minutes.

Meanwhile, soak the bread slices in the egg mixture for about 1 minute on each side. Brush a large baking sheet with the melted butter and place the bread slices on the sheet. Bake in the preheated oven for 5–7 minutes, or until lightly browned. Turn the slices over and bake for a further 2–3 minutes. Serve the berries spooned over the toast and decorated with mint sprigs.

serves 8

125 g/4¹/₂ oz butter, softened,
plus extra for greasing

100 g/3¹/₂ oz caster sugar

55 g/2 oz soft brown sugar

3 eggs

1 tsp vanilla extract

3 large, ripe bananas

250 g/9 oz self-raising flour

1 tsp freshly grated nutmeg

1 tsp ground cinnamon

mascarpone cheese or
natural yogurt, to serve

icing sugar, sifted,
for dusting (optional)

for the strawberry compote

85 g/3 oz soft brown sugar

juice of 2 oranges

grated rind of 1 orange

1 cinnamon stick

400 g/14 oz fresh
strawberries, hulled and
thickly sliced

banana bread with strawberry compote & mascarpone

Preheat the oven to 180°C/350°F/Gas Mark 4. Grease a 23 x 11-cm/ 9 x 4¹/₄-inch loaf tin and line the base with non-stick baking paper.

Put the butter and sugars in a bowl and beat together until light and fluffy. Mix in the eggs, one at a time, then mix in the vanilla extract. Peel the bananas and mash roughly with a fork. Stir gently into the batter mixture, then add the flour, nutmeg and cinnamon, stirring until just combined.

Pour the mixture into the prepared tin and bake in the preheated oven for 1¹/₄ hours, or until a skewer inserted into the centre comes out clean. Leave in the tin for 5 minutes before turning out onto a wire rack to cool.

To make the compote, put the sugar, orange juice and rind and cinnamon stick in a saucepan and bring to the boil. Add the strawberries and return to the boil. Remove from the heat, pour into a clean heatproof bowl and leave to cool. Remove the cinnamon stick. Serve slices of the banana bread with a dollop of mascarpone cheese or yogurt and spoon over the warm or cold compote. Dust with sifted icing sugar if desired.

makes 8 rolls

350 g/12 oz self-raising flour

pinch of salt

2 tbsp caster sugar

1 tsp ground cinnamon

100 g/3$^{1}/_{2}$ oz butter, melted,
plus extra for greasing

2 egg yolks

200 ml/7 fl oz milk,
plus extra for glazing

for the filling

1 tsp ground cinnamon

55 g/2 oz soft brown sugar

2 tbsp caster sugar

1 tbsp butter, melted

for the icing

125 g/4$^{1}/_{2}$ oz icing sugar,
sifted

2 tbsp cream cheese,
softened

1 tbsp butter, softened

about 30 ml/1 fl oz
boiling water

1 tsp vanilla essence

simple cinnamon rolls

Preheat the oven to 180°C/350°F/Gas Mark 4. Grease a 20-cm/8-inch round tin and line the base with baking paper.

Mix the flour, salt, caster sugar and cinnamon together in a large bowl. Whisk the butter, egg yolks and milk together and combine with the dry ingredients to make a soft dough. Turn out onto a large piece of greaseproof paper lightly sprinkled with flour, and roll out to a rectangle 30 x 25 cm/12 x 10 inches.

To make the filling, mix the ingredients together, spread evenly over the dough and roll up, Swiss-roll style, to form a log. Using a sharp knife, cut the dough into 8 even-sized slices and pack into the prepared tin. Brush gently with extra milk and bake for 30–35 minutes, or until golden brown. Remove from the oven and leave to cool for 5 minutes before removing from the tin.

Sift the icing sugar into a large bowl and make a well in the centre. Place the cream cheese and butter in the centre, pour over the water and stir to mix. Add extra boiling water, a few drops at a time, until the icing coats the back of a spoon. Stir in the vanilla essence. Drizzle over the rolls. Serve warm or cold.

makes 12 croissants

500 g/1 lb 2 oz strong white bread flour, plus extra for rolling

40 g/1½ oz caster sugar

1 tsp salt

2 tsp easy-blend dried yeast

300 ml/10 fl oz milk, heated until just warm to the touch

300 g/10½ oz butter, softened, plus extra for greasing

1 egg, lightly beaten with 1 tbsp milk, for glazing

fresh croissants

Preheat the oven to 200°C/400°F/gas mark 6. Stir the dry ingredients into a large bowl, make a well in the centre and add the milk. Mix to a soft dough, adding more milk if too dry. Knead on a lightly floured work surface for 5–10 minutes, or until smooth and elastic. Leave to rise in a large greased bowl, covered, in a warm place until doubled in size. Meanwhile, flatten the butter with a rolling pin between 2 sheets of greaseproof paper to form a rectangle about 5 mm/¼ inch thick, then chill.

Knead the dough for 1 minute. Remove the butter from the refrigerator and leave to soften slightly. Roll out the dough on a well-floured work surface to 46 x 15 cm/18 x 6 inches. Place the butter in the centre, folding up the sides and squeezing the edges together gently. With the short end of the dough towards you, fold the top third down towards the centre, then fold the bottom third up. Rotate 90° clockwise so that the fold is to your left and the top flap towards your right. Roll out to a rectangle and fold again. If the butter feels soft, wrap the dough in clingfilm and chill. Repeat the rolling process twice more. Cut the dough in half. Roll out one half into a triangle 5 mm/¼ inch thick (keep the other half refrigerated). Use a cardboard triangular template, base 18 cm/7 inches and sides 20 cm/8 inches, to cut out the croissants.

Brush the triangles lightly with the glaze. Roll into croissant shapes, starting at the base and tucking the point underneath to prevent unrolling while cooking. Brush again with the glaze. Place on an ungreased baking tray and leave to double in size. Bake for 15–20 minutes until golden brown.

makes 5 x 450-g/1-lb jars

1.6 kg/3 lb 8 oz fresh
strawberries

3 tbsp lemon juice

1.3 kg/3 lb granulated or
preserving sugar

strawberry jam

Preheat the oven to 180°C/350°F/Gas Mark 4. Sterilize five 450 g/
1 lb jam jars with screw-top lids.

Pick over the strawberries and hull – discarding any that are
overripe. Put the fruit in a large saucepan with the lemon juice
and heat over a low heat until some of the fruit juices begin to run.
Continue to simmer gently for 10–15 minutes until softened.

Add the sugar and stir until it has dissolved. Increase the heat and
boil rapidly for 2–3 minutes until setting point is reached. Test the
mixture with a sugar thermometer – it should read 105°C/221°F for
a good setting point. Alternatively, drop a teaspoonful of jam onto
a cold saucer, place it in the refrigerator to cool it, and then push
it with your finger. If it forms a wrinkled skin, it is ready. If not, boil
for a further minute and repeat.

Remove the saucepan from the heat and leave to cool for
15–20 minutes, to prevent the fruit rising in the jar. Skim if
necessary. Meanwhile, warm the jam jars in the preheated oven.
Remove and fill carefully with the jam, using a ladle and a jam
funnel. Top with waxed discs, waxed-side down, and screw on the
lids tightly. Wipe the jars clean and leave to cool. Label and date to
avoid confusion later.

Store in a cool, dry place. Once opened, it is advisable to keep the
jar in the refrigerator.

makes 10

280 g/10 oz self-raising wholemeal flour

2 tsp baking powder

2 tbsp dark muscovado sugar

100 g/3^1/$_2$ oz ready-to-eat dried apricots, finely chopped

1 banana, mashed with 1 tbsp orange juice

1 tsp finely grated orange rind

300 ml/10 fl oz skimmed milk

1 egg, beaten

3 tbsp sunflower oil

2 tbsp rolled oats

fruit spread, honey or maple syrup, to serve

fruity muffins

Preheat the oven to 200°C/400°F/Gas Mark 6. Place 10 paper muffin cases in a muffin tin. Sift the flour and baking powder into a mixing bowl, adding any husks that remain in the sieve. Stir in the sugar and chopped apricots.

Make a well in the centre and add the banana, orange rind, milk, beaten egg and oil. Mix together well to form a thick batter and divide among the muffin cases.

Sprinkle with a few rolled oats and bake in the oven for 25–30 minutes until well risen and firm to the touch or until a cocktail stick inserted into the centre comes out clean.

Remove the muffins from the oven and put them on a wire rack to cool slightly. Serve the muffins while still warm with a little fruit spread, honey or maple syrup.